BALLET

Pointe by Pointe

Missy Mitchell

rosen central™

The Rosen Publishing Group, Inc., New York

Special thanks to Maria DiDia and Sondra Forsyth

Published in 2004 by The Rosen Publishing Group, Inc.
29 East 21st Street, New York, NY 10010

Library of Congress Cataloging-in-Publication Data

Mitchell, Missy.
    Ballet : pointe by pointe / Missy Mitchell.— 1st ed.
    p. cm. — (The curtain call library of dance)
    Summary: Explores the history of ballet, what is involved in becoming a
    ballet dancer, and what to look for when watching a ballet performance.
    ISBN 0-8239-4555-3 (lib. bdg.)
    1. Ballet—Juvenile literature. 2. Ballet dancers—Juvenile
    literature. [1. Ballet. 2. Ballet dancers. 3. Occupations.] I. Title.
    II. Series.

    GV1787.5.M53 2004
    792.8—dc22

                                                       2003011945

Manufactured in the United States of America

CONTENTS

INTRODUCTION

The lights in the theater go down and the audience grows quiet. Behind the curtain, you wait to begin your performance. You've dreamed of this evening for years: You are thinking about all the hard work it took to get you here—years of dance classes, weeks of rehearsals, and many pairs of worn and outgrown pointe shoes and ballet slippers. In the audience, your family and friends eagerly await your appearance.

Quickly, the curtain opens. You make your entrance with a smile. You look as graceful as you feel, wearing your new tutu and pointe shoes. You dance across the stage effortlessly and confidently, knowing that all the time spent practicing and taking care of your body has paid off. Your feeling of joy and happiness grows as the performance goes on. You wish the night could last forever.

One of the most important parts of your work as a ballet dancer is to make your performance look smooth and flawless. Yet it takes years of work to accomplish this great feat. Let's take a look at what you'll need to achieve for the audience to give you a standing ovation!

● Ballet's worldwide popularity has made it the subject of many movies and TV shows. Here, in a scene from the 1977 movie, *The Turning Point*, Mikhail Baryshnikov performs with his partner, Leslie Browne, who is dancing on pointe.

CHAPTER I

BALLET HISTORY

Ballet Beginnings

Ballet as an art form began in the late 1400s, during the Renaissance, in the royal courts of France and Italy. Catherine de Medici, a princess from Italy who married King Henry II of France, was known for throwing large parties where dance and music were performed for royalty.

As the Renaissance continued into the 1600s, France's King Louis XIV turned these parties into lavish court spectacles. King Louis XIV, known as a talented performer, liked to dance. Many of the nobles in the upper class and the military began to study dance and participate in his productions. These performances usually told a mythological story and included music, long heavy costumes, and elaborate sets.

King Louis XIV started the world's first ballet school in 1661. It was during this time that many movements and positions in ballet technique were made standard. These movements and positions, first practiced by people over four hundred years ago, are the same basic steps that you learn in ballet class today. This is why the words you learn for most positions and steps are French!

Getting Romantic

In the early 1800s, a new style of ballet was developed. It was called Romantic ballet. The Romantic period of ballet created many changes. Ballet began to look more like it does today. Costumes became lighter and less restricting. This was the beginning of the idea of a ballet dancer transforming during the dance into a beautiful being from another world. Women dancers began to dance on pointe and performed roles that were graceful and fairy-like. Romantic ballets allowed audiences to escape from the real world into one of fantasy.

As the popularity of ballet began to spread, more changes occurred. More challenging turning and jumping steps were created. Impressive partner work and lifts were added. Different schools of ballet formed in each country. A style of performance and technique became established within each school.

Fun Fact

Pierre Beauchamps, who created dances for Louis XIV (pictured), is credited with defining and naming many of the ballet steps used today.

The Russian Influence

In the late 1800s, ballet emerged as an important art form outside the aristocratic court. Choreographers, or people who create dances, created longer ballets. However, many ballets still had fairy-tale story lines. Ballet companies began to tour around the world. The Ballets Russes was one of the first professional touring dance companies. It was formed in 1909 by the impresario, or producer, Sergei Diaghilev.

As choreographers were given more artistic freedom, they began to experiment with different ideas for ballets. By the early 1900s, works were created that did not follow a specific story line and were more abstract. Some of

Three Styles of Ballet

There are three main styles of ballet: Italian, French, and Russian.

Italian Ballet features strong, dazzling technique. The dancers are known for their ability to execute difficult steps and turns.

French Ballet is known for its elegant, graceful movements over its technical excellence. The influence of the French style of ballet is felt throughout the ballet world.

Russian Ballet contains many steps and movements from both French and Italian styles. It is known for its athleticism and extremes of emotional expression.

these modern ballets, known as neoclassical ballets, were even performed in costumes that look like the simple leotards that you might wear to class.

The Ballets Russes and American Ballet

George Balanchine is generally recognized as the most important person in establishing ballet in America. He was born in 1904 in St. Petersburg, Russia, and trained at the state-sponsored academy from the age of ten. In 1924, he joined Diaghilev's Ballets Russes and soon became chief choreographer. In 1933, the dance patron Lincoln Kirstein hired Balanchine to come to the United States, where they founded the School of American Ballet and the New York City Ballet Company. Balanchine style combines Russian technique with speedy footwork, high leg extensions, pelvic isolations, and even inwardly rotated legs that all reflect the energy and creativity Balanchine felt in America.

Ballet Today

Today, ballet dancers and choreographers continue to be inspired by the world around them. While they continue to perform the great works of the Romantic Era, they are also creating new works, performed to new styles of popular music. When you think about the history of ballet, it is exciting to realize all of the different roles that you could create or perform. One day you could be a fairy princess and the next day you could be a futuristic girl warrior.

● Here, Mikhail Baryshnikov dances with ballerina Gelsey Kirkland in a 1970s TV production of *The Nutcracker*. Baryshnikov choreographed this production for the American Ballet Theatre. Today, Baryshnikov continues to excite dance audiences performing works by modern and post-modern choreographers.

Ballet Dancer Bios

Mikhail Baryshnikov was born in Riga, Latvia, in the former Soviet Union, on June 28, 1948. He began studying ballet at the age of twelve. At nineteen, he was dancing with Russia's famous Kirov Ballet. Baryshnikov defected, or escaped, from the Soviet Union in 1974. He was a member of the American Ballet Theatre and then the New York City Ballet.

Anna Pavlova was born in St. Petersburg, Russia, on February 12, 1881, and trained at the Imperial Ballet School there. Considered one of the greatest classical ballet dancers ever, she is best remembered for her perform-ances of *The Dying Swan,* a solo choreographed by Michel Folkine, that Pavlova danced all over the world.

CHAPTER 2

BALLET CLASS

Dressed for Success

Wearing the proper outfit for class is very important. It shows respect for your teachers and for the art of ballet. It is important to ask your teacher if your dance school has a particular dress code. The most basic outfit is a black leotard, pink tights, and black or pink ballet slippers for girls. Boys wear black tights, white, short-sleeved T-shirts, and white or black slippers. While you may feel self-conscious at first, it is important to wear fitted clothing to class. This will allow you and your teacher to see the lines of your body as you dance.

You should not wear any jewelry to class. Your hair should also be pulled neatly back off your face and neck. This will allow you to perform ballet movements more easily and gracefully.

● Being dressed properly will help you achieve the right attitude for ballet.

Ballet Slippers

Ballet slippers are made from soft leather or canvas and have a thin sole. The slipper is usually held on your foot with a piece of elastic and a drawstring around the top that can be pulled to make the width of the shoe fit tighter. Make sure you either cut off or tuck in the ends of the drawstring—you don't want to trip over anything hanging out of your shoe! Ballet slippers should have a snug fit.

Fun Fact

In ballet, most movements are performed "turned-out." Turned-out is when the legs are rotated out from the hip joints, presenting the inner legs and feet to the audience.

How a Ballet Class Works

You will start the class at the barre. The barre is a horizontal rail, usually made of wood, on which you put your hands or legs when you are doing exercises. It is usually attached to the side of one of the studio's walls, although some studios also have portable barres that are placed in the center of the room. At the barre, you will practice exercises that warm up your muscles and joints.

These exercises will also help you align your bones correctly, stretch and strengthen your muscles, and coordinate the movements of your legs and arms together. The exercises at the barre are also important because they are the fundamental building blocks of all the exciting ballet techniques you will learn.

In the center you will practice port de bras (**pohr duh brah**), literally translated from French as carriage of the arms, or exercises to develop strength and grace in your upper torso, head, and arms. You will also practice adagio (ah-**dazj**-eh-oh), or slow movements, focusing on weight-shifting sequences that include coordinated extensions of your legs and arms, sustained balances, and turns. You will also practice petite

Fun Fact

At the end of class, dancers practice a bow called a révérence. Dancers may think of the bow as thanks to their teachers for what they have learned. It is also customary to applaud your teacher as a thank you at the end of class.

allegro (puh-**teet** ah-**leh**-groh), or quick movements, including small jumps and batterie (bah-**tree**), or beats with the calves and feet.

This work is usually followed by grand allegro (**grahn** ah-**leh**-groh). These exercises focus on bigger leaps, jumps, turns, and the connecting steps that move

● Every ballet class begins with exercises at the barre. The barre provides a gentle support for the subtle weight shifts that occur early in the lesson as the dancers stretch and strengthen their muscles. Barre exercises are important to a dancer's development.

you from one end of the dance floor to the other. Your ability to perform these fun and exciting movements across the floor will be directly related to how well you perform the exercises at the barre.

Taking Corrections

Ballet requires a great amount of self-discipline. You have to stay focused in class and practice hard every chance you get. Your teacher is there to help guide you through this process. He or she will demonstrate movements as you watch and listen carefully. Then you will do them.

It is important for teachers to give corrections during class. This will help you be a better dancer. Listen to your teacher's corrections and keep them in mind as you practice. If there is something that you don't understand, ask your teacher to explain it to you.

Dealing With Frustration

There will be times in class when you might have a hard time with steps that other dancers may perform easily. Feeling upset about this is natural. While you may feel frustrated, there are ways you can help yourself feel better. Remember the things you do really well in class. This will help you keep a positive outlook. Try not to get angry or jealous of another student for doing something well. Instead, give him or her a compliment or ask how he or she does it! Your classmate will probably be very happy to give you some tips. If someone else asks you for help, take it as a compliment.

The Importance of Music

Ballet is a classical art form. It is most often performed to classical music. Bars of music are arranged in measures. You can tell how the beat of the music is counted by the time signature. Time signatures tell you how many beats are in every measure of music. Rhythms tell you the length of the musical note. Dancers count their steps to the music according to how many beats are in each measure and the length of each note.

Beyond Classical

Many ballets include music and dance that is inspired by other dance forms. Here is a sampling of some music and dance styles that have become part of ballet:

Polonaise (poh-leh-**naze**) is a presentational dance that began in Poland in the seventeenth century. *Swan Lake* and *The Sleeping Beauty* are two ballets that feature polonaise.

Mazurka (muh-**zuhr**-kuh) is a Polish folk dance that has found its way into ballet. It features the stamping of feet and the clicking of heels. Mazurka has been used in many classical ballets including *Coppélia*.

Tango (**tang**-go) is a South American social dance for couples. Tango has been featured in many ballets such as *Façade* and *Souvenirs*.

CHAPTER 3

YOUR BODY IS A TOOL

Listening to Your Body

Listening to your body is an important overall skill to have as a dancer. Your body will tell you when it needs help. It is important not to ignore the messages your body is sending you. Hunger is your body telling you that it needs more energy. When a part of your body hurts, it is trying to tell you that it is working too hard, or working incorrectly and needs rest and attention.

Healthy Eating

One of the best ways to keep your body healthy is through good eating habits. Your body uses a lot of energy when you dance. Don't skip meals throughout the day. However, don't eat a huge meal before

you take class either. It will make you feel full and tired. Instead, be sure to eat some healthy snacks throughout the day before you dance to give you energy. Afterward, have a larger meal that includes all the important vitamins, minerals, and proteins that you need.

Although it is tempting to eat snacks with a high amount of fats and sugars, they're not good for you. When you snack on things like chips and candy, your body only gets a very temporary burst of energy and you will feel tired more quickly afterward.

Importance of Water

Your body will lose a lot of fluid when you sweat from all

● To stay fit and healthy, ballet dancers need to eat plenty of fresh fruits and vegetables.

the hard work you are doing while you are dancing. Drinking water is the best way to keep your body hydrated. You should drink at least eight glasses of water a day. Fruit and vegetable juices are another good choice. Stay away from drinks that have a lot of artificial sugars and caffeine, like sodas. Caffeine actually dehydrates your body. Too much sugar will make you tired.

Dancers' Hygiene

Although you will walk into class feeling clean and put together, that won't be the case by the time you leave. Some extra deodorant will help keep you smelling fresh while you dance. A hot shower or bath will keep you clean and will also soothe your muscles after a long day of dancing. You should also pay special attention to your feet, especially when you begin dancing on pointe. Keep your

Before-Class Snacks

For a light meal before class or a quick energy boost that's healthy, try:

Yogurt and granola
Soups and salads
Raw fruits and vegetables
Sandwiches with protein fillings like cheese or peanut butter

toenails clipped evenly and at a short length. Be sure to keep any cuts you have on your feet clean and bandaged.

Dealing With Injuries

Even dancers who practice with the proper technique sometimes get injured. Common injuries for dancers occur in their feet, ankles, knees, and back. Many of these injuries, like sprains and strains, can heal in about a week's time if you rest. If you are more seriously injured, you may not be able to dance for a little while, and this can be upsetting. However, dancing with an injury can make the problem worse and will

● Proper warm-ups that include gentle stretching can help dancers reduce their risk of injuries. Muscles that are not sufficiently warmed up and loosened are more likely to be pulled or torn.

● Balancing a busy dance schedule with homework can be a real challenge. Plan your time carefully so that you'll succeed both in class and on the dance floor.

keep you off your feet even longer. Once you are healed, pay special attention to the part of the body that was injured. Some exercises might be a little painful at first. If something hurts too much, don't feel pressured to do it right away. As long as you listen to your body and follow the advice of your doctor, teacher, and parents, you should be dancing better than ever in a short time.

Physical Changes

As you get older and your body changes and grows, you might find that your body starts to feel different when you are dancing. Some things that used to be easy to do may suddenly be difficult. Don't worry. Different parts of your body grow at different rates and it will take some time for your body to get used to its new coordinations. While this may seem frustrating, it is important to know that your body is just doing what it needs to do to make you a healthy adult.

Balancing Ballet Classes and Schoolwork

It is important to plan your time between school and dance class carefully so that you can give your best to everything you do. Being a student and a dancer requires a lot of physical and mental energy. You may be more tired than usual on days when you are dancing. Plan extra time for studying and homework on the days when you are not in dance class.

CHAPTER 4

GOING ON POINTE

Pointe dancing in ballet refers to dancing on the tips of the toes. This very difficult technique requires special shoes that allow the dancer to balance her body weight on a tiny flat surface. It takes a great amount of hard work to wear these special shoes. There are many skills that you must master in order to support the weight of your whole body on your toes.

Working Toward Pointe

Dancers usually start pointe work around the age of ten or twelve. When you are younger, the bones in your feet are still soft. Your feet can become damaged if you dance on pointe before they are fully grown and solid.

Your teacher will tell you when you are ready to wear pointe shoes.

Fun Fact

Many believe that Marie Taglioni (pictured) was one of the first dancers to dance on pointe. She did so in the 1832 production of La Sylphide.

● Dancing on pointe is a lot of hard work but also a joyous experience for ballet dancers.

Pointe Shoes

Pointe shoes are made so that a dancer can perform all kinds of movements in one pair of shoes. Although pointe shoes look delicate on the outside because of a pink satin covering, the inside of the shoe is actually very stiff. The part of the shoe on which a dancer balances is called the box. The area around it is reinforced with a plasterlike material. To maintain balance for long periods of time, there is a stiff piece of material in the sole of the shoe called the shank.

Proper Fit

When it is time to get your first pair of pointe shoes, it is important to go to a footwear professional who can fit them properly on your feet. There are many different kinds of pointe shoes. Some shoes are made especially for dancers who are just starting out. You should ask your teacher if there is a particular kind that he or she would like you to wear.

Pointe shoes are supposed to fit snugly and may not feel comfortable. If your shoes are too big you might hurt yourself when you are dancing. When you are standing flat in your shoes, your toes should touch the tip without curling around each other. Your feet are more compact when you are on your toes, so when you balance on pointe, there should be a little bit of extra fabric in the back of the shoe. Always have your teacher check the fit of your first pair of pointe shoes before attaching ribbons and elastic.

● To avoid injuries or stumbling while dancing, it is important to tie your pointe shoes properly.

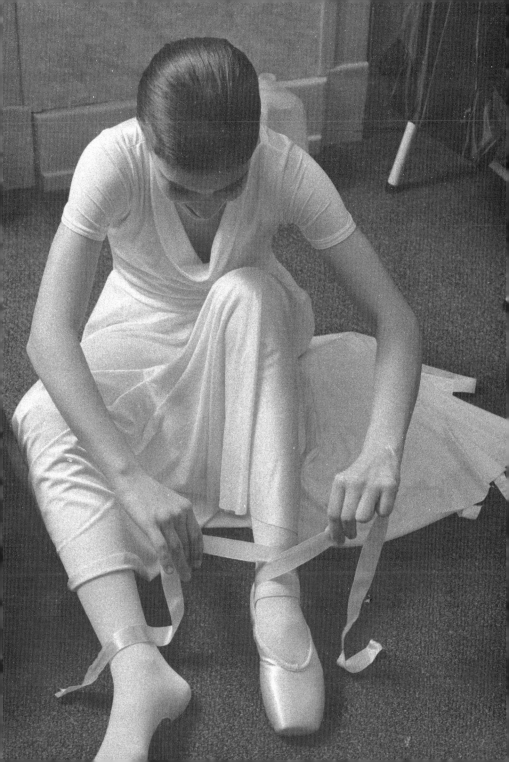

Preparing Your Shoes

Once you have found the perfect fit, you will need to outfit your shoes with the right padding and ribbons. Your teacher will help you pick the padding that's right for you. She will also show you how to sew on your ribbons and elastic.

Although you will be excited when you get your first pair of pointe shoes, it is important not to dance in them until you get to class. At first, you will only wear your shoes for a few minutes at the barre. As time goes on, you will wear them for more of the barre work. Then, when you are strong enough, you will practice steps in the center of the room.

● Ballet teachers help students learn proper body placement.

Practicing at home will help keep you on your toes during class. It might be tempting to try a daring balance or spin when nobody is looking, but you could hurt yourself. Instead, practice the exercises you do at the barre. This will help keep your feet and ankles strong and healthy.

Good Pain, Bad Pain

Dancing on pointe might be harder than you imagined. Your shoes might feel uncomfortable. Your feet will probably hurt. Eventually, your shoes will become softer and form to fit your feet. A little bit of pain is completely normal, because your feet are using all of their muscles and strength to help you balance on your toes. The tops of your toes might even develop blisters from rubbing against the stiff material inside the shoe.

While a little bit of pain is okay, if something in your feet or ankles hurts badly or the pain doesn't go away, talk to your teacher. He or she can tell you if the pain you are experiencing is normal and can probably suggest a solution. Dancing on pointe should be fun and you should feel good in your pointe shoes.

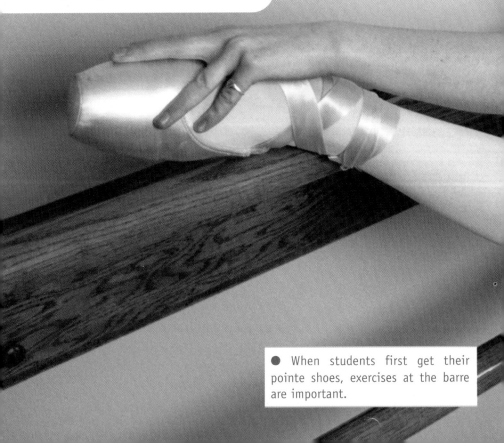

● When students first get their pointe shoes, exercises at the barre are important.

CHAPTER 5

WATCHING THE BALLET

Watching a ballet is fun. You have probably heard of some great classic ballets already, such as *The Nutcracker, The Sleeping Beauty,* and *Swan Lake.* Different dance companies often use different costumes, sets, and even steps to tell these classic stories. Before you view a performance, do some research to learn about the story or the history of its performances.

Paying Attention

There are many things to notice when you go to a performance. The most obvious thing you'll see, of course, is the dancing! As you watch the ballet, try to identify some of the steps that the dancers are doing. You will be happy to notice that you have performed many of those steps yourself! Watch how the dancers portray a particular character. Also take in the sets and lighting and listen to the music.

Costumes

Besides the dancing, one of the most beautiful things about the ballet is the costumes. Costumes help dancers become different characters. They also help to highlight the energy and line of the movement. Classical ballet costumes are usually more elaborate than neoclassical costumes. They often include the most famous piece of ballet wear—the tutu.

● Many different ballet companies have performed *Swan Lake*. Here, a ballet company from Russia performs *Swan Lake* at the Edinburgh International Festival in Scotland.

Ballet Stories

Swan Lake, one of the most famous and popular ballets ever created, is a four-act ballet originally choreographed by Julius Reisinger to music by Peter Ilich Tchaikovsky. It premiered on March 4, 1877, at the Bolshoi Theatre in Moscow. However, it was not well received. It was later revised, first by Joseph Hansen in 1880 and 1882, and then by Marius Petipa and Lev Ivanov in 1895. The Petipa-Ivanova version became the definitive version of *Swan Lake*. The ballet is based on a German folk tale and tells the story of a princess who is turned into a swan by a magician. The only way she can be turned back into a human is if a man swears his true love to her.

Fancy Free is a one-act ballet that was choreographed by Jerome Robbins. It premiered on April 19, 1944. It was staged by Ballet Theatre at the Metropolitan Opera House in New York City. The ballet is about the adventures of three U.S. Navy sailors on leave in New York City during World War II. It was an instant hit and went on to influence not only ballet, but theater and movies. *Fancy Free* was turned into the popular movie musical *On the Town*, which was also choreographed by Robbins. Both shows featured music by Leonard Bernstein.

Makeup

Ballet dancers put the finishing touches on their beautiful images with their hair and makeup. If you saw a ballet dancer in stage makeup up close, you would see that he or she is wearing much more than what 'people usually wear on the street. Some dancers perform in huge theaters with seats that stretch far away from the stage. By wearing makeup that makes his or her facial features, such as eyes, look larger than usual, a dancer's facial expressions can be seen even by audience members sitting in the back row of the theater. Finishing touches can include hair accessories like flowers or a tiara.

A Career in Ballet

Studying ballet and watching great dancers perform might inspire you to think seriously about becoming a ballet dancer. In order to become a professional, you'll need to do a lot of work! Professional ballet dancers take class every day and spend even more time in rehearsals or practicing on their own.

Most ballet dancers start planning their careers in their teens. To consider ballet as a career, you should take at least three classes per week. You will need to give extra time to rehearsals and performances.

Many young dancers spend summers at dance camps, or "intensives," where they study ballet all day. Some dancers even attend arts high schools, where they take ballet and study other subjects all in the same school.

Getting serious about ballet is a big choice to make. It is

● Ballet dancers take great care when applying their makeup. Here, prima ballerina Nina Anaiashvili puts on her makeup before a performance. Fellow dancer Andriti Liepa looks on.

helpful to talk to your dance teachers and parents when you are considering this kind of decision. Your teacher can help you decide if it's a proper career choice for you and can assist you in finding opportunities that might be right for you. Ballet is a truly wonderful activity to be a part of and with hard work and dedication, one day you might find yourself center stage dancing on pointe and taking a curtain call!

Ballet Jobs

If you love ballet, but choose not to be a performer, there are many careers that involve dance where you can explore other skills and interests. Here is a list of some important jobs that can be found in the world of ballet:

Choreographer
Costume or Set Designer
Dance Company Manager
Dance Critic
Dance Teacher
Doctor or Physical Therapist for Dancers

GLOSSARY

barre (**bar**) The horizontal pole, usually made of wood, used as a handrail by ballet dancers to maintain balance as they exercise.

choreographers (kor-ee-**og**-ruh-furz) People who create ideas and movements for a ballet.

corrections (kuh-**rekt**-shuhnz) Comments given by a person, such as a ballet teacher, in order to help a student improve his or her work.

hydrated (hye-**drate**-uhd) To drink water or other fluids that allow the body to function properly.

hygiene (**hye**-jeen) Actions taken by people to stay healthy and keep clean.

intensives (in-**tenss**-ihvz) Camps that teach ballet.

leotard (**lee**-uh-tard) A one-piece garment worn for dancing or exercise.

measures (**mezh**-urz) Bars of music.

pointe (**point**) Dancing on the tips of the toes.

pointe shoes (**point shooz**) Shoes worn by ballet dancers to dance on pointe; made specially to allow the dancer to balance her entire bodyweight on a tiny flat surface.

Renaissance (**ren**-uh-sahnss) The revival of art and learning in Europe between the fourteenth and sixteenth centuries.

rhythms (**rith**-uhmz) Regular beats in music, poetry, or dance.

Romantic ballet (roh-**man**-tik **bal**-lay) A style of ballet that was popular in the 1830s and 1840s; many romantic ballets dealt with supernatural or fantasy themes.

royalty (**roi**-uhl-tee) People belonging to the family of a king or queen.

technique (tek-**neek**) A method or way of doing something that requires skill.

time signatures (**time sig**-nuh-churz) Signs used in music to indicate meter, usually written as fractions.

tutu (**too**-too) A ballet skirt made of several layers of tulle, or stiff netting.

FOR MORE INFORMATION

Organizations

Royal Academy of Dance
36 Battersea Square
London SW11 3RA
United Kingdom
+44 (0)20 7326 8000
Web site: http://www.radacadabra.org

School of American Ballet
70 Lincoln Center Plaza
New York, NY 10023-6592
(212) 769-6600
Web site: http://www.sab.org

Web Sites

Due to the changing nature of Internet links, the Rosen Publishing Group, Inc., has developed an online list of Web sites related to the subject of this book. This site is updated regularly. Please use this link to access the list:

http://www.rosenlinks.com/ccld/ballet/

FOR FURTHER READING

Books

Augustyn, Frank, and Shelley Tanaka. *Footnotes: Dancing the World's Best-Loved Ballets*. Brookfield, CT: Millbrook Press, 2001.

Barringer, Janice, and Sarah Schlesinger. *The Pointe Book: Shoes, Training and Technique*. Hightstown, NJ: Princeton Book Company Publishers, 1998.

Bowes, Deborah. *The Ballet Book: The Young Performer's Guide to Classical Dance*. Toronto, ON, Canada: Firefly Books, Ltd, 1999.

Kristy, Davida. *George Balanchine: American Ballet Master*. Minneapolis, MN: Lerner Publishing Group, 1996.

Martins, Peter. *The New York City Ballet Workout: Fifty Stretches and Exercises Anyone Can Do for a Strong, Graceful, and Sculpted Body*. New York: William Morrow & Company, 1997.

Magazines and Publications

Curtain Call Dance Club Revue
P.O. Box 709
York, PA 17405-0709
Web site: http://www.cckids.com

Dance
333 7th Avenue, 11th floor
New York, NY 10001
(212) 979-4803
Web site: http://www.dancemagazine.com

Dancer
2829 Bird Avenue, Suite 5PMB 231
Miami, FL 33133
(305) 460-3225
Web site: http://www.danceronline.com

Pointe Magazine
Lifestyle Ventures, LLC
250 West 57th Street, Suite 420
New York, NY 10107
(212) 265-8890
Web site: http://www.pointemagazine.com

BIBLIOGRAPHY

"Ballet." World Book Online, Americas ed., Retrieved May 2003 (subscription service)

"Ballet." Encyclopedia Britannica Online, Retrieved May 2003 (subscription service)

"Ballets Russes." World Book Online Americas Edition, Retrieved May 2003 (subscription service)

Craine, Debra, and Judith Mackrell. *The Oxford Dictionary of Dance*. New York: Oxford University Press, 2002.

Grant, Gail. *Technical Manual and Dictionary of Classical Ballet*. New York: Dover Publications, Inc., 1982.

Greskovic, Robert. *Ballet 101: A Complete Guide to Learning and Loving the Ballet*. Collingdale: PA, Diane Publishing Company, 2000.

Lourdou, Dorothy. "Sergei Pavlovich Diaghilev." World Book Online Americas Edition. Retrieved May 2003 (subscription service)

Matheson, Katy. "George Balanchine." World Book Online Americas Edition. Retrieved May 2003 (subscription service)

"Mazurka." Encyclopedia Britannica Online. Retrieved May 2003 (subscription service)

Odom, Selma Landen. "Bolshoi." World Book Online Americas Edition. Retrieved May 2003 (subscription service)

"Polonaise." Encyclopedia Britannica Online. Retrieved May 2003 (subscription service)

"Rhythm." Encyclopedia Britannica Online. Retrieved May 2003 (subscription service)

"Tango." Encyclopedia Britannica Online. Retrieved May 2003 (subscription service)

"Time Signature." Encyclopedia Britannica Online. Retrieved May 2003 (subscription service)

INDEX

About the Author

Missy Mitchell received her B.S. and M.A. from New York University in Dance and Dance Education. She is a dancer, teacher, choreographer, and writer who lives in New York City.

Editor: Eric Fein **Book Design:** Christopher Logan and Erica Clendening
Developmental Editors: Nancy Allison, CMA, RME, and Susan Epstein